Life,
Spirit,
and You
"The Alpha Train"

Gail J. Chiasson

TABLE OF CONTENTS

ACKNOWLEDGEMENTS

I would like to thank my family and friends for all of your support throughout the writing and production of my work. A special thank you goes out to my husband Marty who supported me unconditionally.

DEDICATION

*I dedicate this book to my Mom
who taught me the greatest lesson in life:
Be a free spirit!
Dance when you can;
Laugh when you can;
Eat what you like but not too much;
Let your spirit give of yourself to others.
People in life are important, not possessions.*

Edna (Agnes) Garbien

09.07.1920 to 08.28.2010

INTRODUCTION

This inspirational, motivational, and holistic book was written to create a network of camaraderie amongst women to help relieve the feeling of loneliness, isolation, prejudice, and unfairness in personal and professional situations.

As you read about each person in Life, Spirit, and You, there may be a situation or personal trait that might be like yourself or someone you know. We are all in life together and need to feel that we are not alone. These are short stories to take with you on the bus, train, or maybe even to the airport. Following most of the chapters, is an area for your own personal notes. You might have been in or heard of a similar situation, please take a moment to reflect how you reacted or dealt with it. The last chapter is to be written by you, for you.

Throughout my life, I have always been creative, and writing a book was a way to leave a trace of my thoughts and adventures with others. Hopefully, someday this will build a network to keep the help and caring going. So sit back and turn the page.

A lter thought processes of eating.

B e strong when choosing your food.

B arely eat unhealthy foods.

E njoy eating to live; not living to eat.

Y our eating habit of today is a picture of what you will look like tomorrow.

Chapter One

ABBEY

Abbey was born of farmer parents both of who were very handsome and beautiful. She and her parents lived in Falls Church, VT. Abbey was a petite young lady, twelve years old. She had big brown eyes, chestnut color hair, and skin like peaches and cream. Her story and turmoil in life was that being brought up with farmer parents, they were old fashioned in many ways. She wanted to be modernized but her parents were stuck in the early 1900's when in fact, it was almost the year of the millennium 2000.

She went to school in hand-smocked dresses, ankle socks, and Mary Jane shoes (shoes with the strap across the ankle). Although she was beautiful, the kids in school made fun of her. They especially made fun of her when her Dad would drive her to school in his bright red dump truck. Her mom Bonnie was a homemaker who was always very busy with her chores such as feeding the animals, cooking home-made dinners, sewing, painting, and cleaning.

Abbey loved her parents but needed to be modernized so the kids would not laugh and call her "farmer girl." She dreamt of turning thirteen and finally being a teenager.

When the day arrived, she cut and permanent waved her beautiful straight hair, bought some mini-skirts, chunky shoes, and figured out how to put on a push-up bra. The kids in high school were going to know a different Abbey in September.

September came and Abbey got dressed for school and realized that her mini-skirts that she purchased did not fit. They were now too tight. She had put on weight over the summer and didn't realize it. Even the bra was too small. What happened? Abbey ate ice cream and didn't ride her bike over the summer and put on thirty pounds. Wow!

Dieting became a norm and took her from one mood swing to another. Abbey hated her fat self and soon did everyone around her. It took her until she was eighteen years old to stabilize her diet with a normal weight. Soon her parents had to wake up and get into the 19th century before they lost her.

As life came with its challenges, Abbey controlled her eating habit and never put weight on again. Abbey made a life change early in her life and stayed true to herself. She was on the right track and became a nutritionist to help other people with eating disorders.

PERSONAL NOTES

B rainstorm inventive ways to make money.

E nsure healthy vision through regular check-ups with your physician.

T each yourself to be independent and prosperous.

T rain yourself to learn a trade.

Y ield to challenging physical impairment issues and try to move forward.

Chapter Two

BETTY

Betty Johnson was a seamstress who had been sewing since she was four and one-half years old. She was thirty-seven years old and lived in Hailey, ID. Betty was old-fashioned looking with long hair (not colored and half gray) that she wore in a beau font and bun. On the small side, she carried the hairdo off elegantly and gracefully. She spoke very soft and gentle. Her mother and father didn't know how to sew. Betty had no idea how she picked up that skill so young! It appears that she always knew how to sew.

Betty had her own tailoring business called "The Stitchery." She also enjoyed collecting interesting and exotic fabrics. Betty and her sister Marissa traveled often in the United States and on occasion to Europe. Money was always an issue with Betty who worked long hours and was lucky to earn enough money to pay her monthly bills. Marissa, her sister, married into a family with money. Money was never an issue with Marissa but loneliness was. She often wanted to pay Betty's way, but Betty would not accept it.

On a brisk September morning, Betty finished an intricate quilt that she had been working on for three years.

She decided to have it framed and hung in the foyer of her home. If anything, it was a conversation piece. Marissa would go around town bragging about what a great looking quilt her sister made.

Betty had an eye doctor's appointment one Thursday morning for her usual check-up. She was told some startling news. Betty's doctor told her that she had a rare eye disease. Along with the aging process, her vision was deteriorating at a faster pace than most people because of sewing and looking at the fine stitches. The doctor said that she might have to give up sewing because she may go blind. She was devastated! Upset and crying, she drove home in tears only to look around to appreciatively treasure the blue sky, the green trees, the white fluffy clouds, and her little red brick home. Betty called Marissa to tell her the news. Marissa was upset and drove over to Betty's home to be with her. How will Betty support herself? She needed her eyes so she could sew.

Days turned into months and months turned into years. Betty's eyesight diminished slowly. She began to teach herself how to sew quilts with her eyes almost closed. She sold these beautiful handcrafted quilts to a famous store. Betty gave up tailoring clothing and took on custom quilt making.

Marissa set Betty up with a Financial Advisor to invest some of her newly earned money. She has been stable for five years so far and can still see with very strong glasses. She continues to make custom quilts to support herself. Betty laid the groundwork as an example and a good foundation to teach others that you can still be independent and self-supporting even with a disability.

PERSONAL NOTES

C hannel energy to eliminate the need for addiction.

L imit destructive behavior.

A dd happiness to your life by loving yourself first.

I nterest yourself in loving and inspiring bursts of positive ambition.

R eward yourself with healthy and fun holistic care.

E volve a new you every so often; learn, grow, and love who you are every step of the way.

Chapter Three

CLAIRE

Claire loved to smoke. She was forty-five years old with short brown hair that was bleached blond. She lived in Dallas, TX. She also had a raspy voice and a tough attitude. She worked for many different companies and once was the supervisor of a clerical staff. She often liked to smoke, play cards on the computer, play poker with her friends, and eat snacks that were not very healthy for her. She loved her two families who were from her first and second husbands. She also loved having all the families together at the holidays. Her holidays were her precious moments. She enjoyed having everyone together and tasting all the delicious food that she would prepare.

Claire decided in order to make more money that she would go to college so she could get a higher paying job. So she signed up, went to school in the evening for four years, and decided to change her life in a positive way.

If you asked her how she was doing, she would answer, "I'm fine, you know, just doing." Claire's dilemma was in question. Did she really need to smoke so often? Every fifteen minutes or so Claire would light up another cigarette.

She called it, "Networking at school and work." She'd come back with the latest gossip and what not. She didn't appear to eat balanced meals although she did cook them. Her cigarettes kept her balanced.

In June, she graduated from college at age forty-nine. She finally did it! For a graduation present, her husband Andrew gave her a two-week vacation at a stop-smoking ranch in Arizona. She thought that she was going to die at the ranch, but made it through the days. Claire tried to give up smoking. The counselors also put her on a vegetarian diet. Claire was fine at the stop-smoking ranch and came home with a positive attitude. Both families were going to be proud of her!

Claire started job searching because being an Administrative Assistant was starting to get boring. She wanted to try to use her Bachelor Degree in Psychology to aide elderly people in a convalescent home. Claire rewrote her resume with her new degree and sent a few of them out.

Claire got a call to go on an interview and she went. She got the job as assistant manager of counseling for geriatrics at the Walnut Grove Home. Claire got a substantial raise in salary compared to her administrative assistant position. She really loved helping the older people out. But as days wore on, she got tired and took a drag from a cigarette after she ate her lunch. She had a rough morning as an older woman started crying how she missed her family and it was hard for Claire. No one visited this woman and no one cared. Claire took her job seriously and slowly started smoking again as she thought it relaxed her and helped her get through the day.

One day Claire did not wake up and died at home. Her death report analyzed that she died of lung cancer. But didn't Claire know? She should have been knowledgeable enough to know the symptoms.

Claire's dilemma was, "Did she really need all of those cigarettes along with not taking care of herself physically and nutritionally?" She took care of everyone else but herself. All that life has to offer and possibly more to come. But the question remains, "Did the cigarettes kill her (her addicted joy) or was she going to pass away anyway?" Did she live her life in happiness and do we have the right to question?

PERSONAL NOTES

D ream of living
your life as if it was
your last.

O rder your life as you
want it; you have only
one life!

R eview career goals
and modify when
necessary.

A sk your spirit from
within, What will
make ME happy?

Chapter Four

DORA

Dora lived in Katonah, NY and worked in New York City. She was a jazz and tap dancer since she was nine years old and was thirty-seven years old. She had to quit dancing because of problems with her feet. She always thought that she would make it on Broadway but her feet did not go with the flow of things. She was married to a fireman named Tom. Tom and Dora had a teenage boy that was thirteen years old and a teenage girl that was fifteen years old. Their daughter lived at a private school in Connecticut while their son went to a public school in Katonah and lived at home with his parents.

It was damp day in New York City. Floods and flood related problems happened all day. Subways were stopped because of flooding. It was a very messy site. As the companies let employees out at different times, people were taking trains and cabs to get out of the city.

Dora was catching her evening train to go home and was very talkative and involved in the happenings of the train. She went on and on about the flooding. Her day ended when she tried to get back home to the suburbs in Katonah, NY. When she got off the train, she tried to get a cab. No cabs would take any more jobs because of the flooding. She tried to call home and only got the answering machine. So, Dora decided to walk home. It was the only way to get there. She walked four miles of which the last two were flooded with at least two and one-half feet of water. Needless to say, Dora was wading for two miles to try to get back home.

Dora usually wore sneakers when she walked because she had problems with her feet. Her feet had large corns on her toes and bunions on the sides of her feet. Her podiatrist did little to relieve the pain and discomfort that she always was experiencing. She walked in the cold water treading every inch of the way to get home. She thought that maybe she wouldn't make it. She hadn't had any food since the morning and she had gotten cold and weak. Thoughts of dying had crossed her mind and all she kept thinking about was her husband, son, and daughter. The pain she experienced with her feet was painstakingly sharp and piercing. Thoughts of home and safety drifted in and out of her mind.

As she neared her home, she saw lights on. That was a good sign that someone was home. When she walked in to say that she finally made it home from the treacherous journey from work, no one acknowledged her! Her son and her husband were fast asleep on the couch with the TV blasting. Left over Chinese food was carelessly left on the table. They had eaten take-out Chinese food and then had fallen fast asleep on the couch watching TV. Dora was in tears and fled to her bedroom!

Dora had given up her career as a dancer to be a physician's assistant. She made a decent salary to carry her husband's enormous charge account bills. He would think nothing of charging twenty-five dollars for lunch. As a fireman in his hometown, he didn't make a king's salary to support his lifestyle. No one cared or was worried about Dora's safety on this horrible day. Dora carried the financial burden of the household as well as the physical pain and discomfort of her feet.

As a physician's assistant, Dora assisted doctors in outpatient surgery and had a tedious job. She loved her work but always wondered what it have been like if she became a famous dancer. After the incident with the flood, Dora woke up and decided it was time to change her lifestyle. Instead of commuting into NYC for a high salary, she decided to get a job at her local hometown hospital for less pay. She also decided to volunteer at the high school and assisted the dance teacher with teaching the theory of dance to the high school students. Her husband Tom got a reality check about his spending habits. He soon learned how to make peanut butter and jelly sandwiches for lunch. Dora's daughter had to stop attending the private expensive school in Connecticut and enrolled in the free public school in Katonah. Life was changed and it sure was different! Dora's family had to make some major adjustments to their lifestyle in order to accommodate Dora's lesser paying job. She enjoyed her new job at the hospital and the volunteer job at the high school. Dora's family realized that maybe they were too spoiled and looked at life differently now. Meanwhile Dora too changed her outlook on life. She woke up to the tune that living a fulfilled life is living every day as if it were your last.

PERSONAL NOTES

E njoy each stage of your life; enrich it with things you carry around but not to ignore those things that can't be put in your bag.

L ofty dreams of life and spirit create "Out of the bag thinking."

S implicity brings clarity for choosing which items we can toss out and which items we still need to work on and to carry in our baggage.

I magine the collection of bags over a lifetime; "Do you have any bags to let go of?"

E nvelop your moments of time in your heart; this is an endless place with no bags to carry but only to live and love.

Chapter Five

ELSIE

Elsie was a strong beautiful lady with a confession. She was fifty-three years old and lived in Chicago, IL. She doesn't know when it happened. That is, it was her addiction to bags. She thinks it happened somewhere between diapers and kindergarten but the exact time was not known.

Going back to when Elsie was a baby, she always knew that something was good in that diaper bag! Formula and her favorite blanket were in mother's bag and when Elsie and her mother would go out of the house, her mother would bring "the bag." As life progressed into grade school, Elsie loved getting a new lunch bag and book bag every year. She was on her way into becoming a bag lady. As the grades increased, so did her books in the book bag. This bag was getting heavier and heavier.

When Elsie turned thirteen years old, she started carrying another bag. It contained all her personal items such as lip-gloss, eye make-up, comb, tissues, mirror, wallet, and other personal items. Now Elsie's bags added up to three: lunch bag, book bag, and purse. On days that Elsie had to go to cheerleading practice, she brought her gym bag. She was able to consolidate by putting her purse in the gym bag. Now she was up to four bags! Wow! Elsie used to chuckle to herself on how she was the "bag lady!"

When Elsie graduated high school, she got a job at the local dairy on an assembly line during the day and went to college at night. She still chuckled about being the bag lady as she still had the lunch and book bag but now another bag contained college books! Elsie carried her bags throughout her whole school career and then some.

At age twenty-four she married Bob and soon they had three children and yes! More bags! Diaper bags and day bags were added to Elsie's collection. Some bags were more organized than others, but the carrying of bags never stopped.

When Elsie's children were in middle school and high school, her bags were considerably less than in previous years. However, when in her forties, her children reached college age, she noticed that her bags increased again. She now cared for her parents in a senior citizen home and carried a thermal bag of home cooked soup and goodies for them. She also did the same when she went to visit the children in college. The "bag lady" still holds the title!

Now Elsie turned fifty-three and at this age, she finds that she still needs to carry bags. Elsie's left shoulder hurts when she drapes a shoulder strap over it. She carries a purse, lunch bag, and her craft bag to work. Not to mention her gym bag packed in the car to go to exercise class at the gym after work and an emergency bag in the trunk. Elsie contemplates about her shoulder problems which were probably due from carrying bags. A lifetime of lugging bags has taken its toll. But Elsie confesses privately that when it is time for her angels to take her, she smiles and chuckles, she'll have to say, "Wait a moment, I have to get my bag!"

PERSONAL NOTES

F ind your spirit from within.... repair your friendship with yourself, your toughest critic!

R ead as much as you can and try to remember what you read when you are talking to people.

A dvance yourself with new possibilities, challenges, and goals.

N ever forget you are worth it!

C hange things about yourself that you don't like gradually.

E mploy books to be your teachers and friends.

S hare thoughts and dreams of positive goals and ambitions.

Chapter Six

FRANCES

Frances was a stocky young lady around thirty-four years old who was divorced with one boy around eleven years old who lived in Morristown, NJ. She learned to type from taking a night course at her local high school. She wore clothes from the second hand store and would accessorize her outfits nicely to make the most use out of them.

Frances was a clerk typist at a small factory that made sneakers and often would speak about bettering herself through education. Often when confronted with why doesn't she sign up at a local college and take a course, she would reply, "I can't take away what little time I have with my son as my ex-husband never even calls. My boy needs me and I need him." She was happy to have a job and be able to support her apartment and her boy.

Frances liked to ask questions to other assistants at work such as, "How old can you be when you take a course? I guess I'm too old. There must be all young kids at the school."

Lay-offs started at the sneaker factory, and another administrative assistant who just graduated with an Associate Degree moved on to another department. She often encouraged Frances to sit and teach herself the programs on the computer in her spare time at work when things got slow at the work. Well a year and a few months went by and the person who had moved on called Frances to see how things were. She found out some good and bad things. Frances's apartment got robbed, ransacked and completely damaged. No one was hurt during the robbery at her apartment. She took a course or two and passed the classes much to her surprise. Her son got a scholarship and got accepted to a private high school because of his academic achievement and his community leadership.

Another year went by and the person who seemed to always be on the move came to visit Frances to say "Goodbye." She was moving on to another company altogether with her Bachelor of Science degree and the hope and promise of good things to come. Frances, on the other hand, was content to be a secretary (now that she got promoted). Her son had done well and Frances even started to date a young man in her English 101 class. Her new boyfriend even gets along with son who needed a father figure for a long time. Frances had to get going as someone in her group was asking her a question. She said to the person saying goodbye, "You know something, if you didn't leave your job, I would have been laid off a long time ago. They consolidated departments and I have some of your old responsibilities." Hey by the way, however you designed the department's filing system it works great! I never changed a thing and its works. Thanks. Oh, by the way, good luck! Oh, and when I think about it, if you didn't move on, I wouldn't have a job!"

PERSONAL NOTES

G ood thing things are
learned from challenging
relationships.

I nvolve yourself in your
OWN LIFE.

N ever give up; you will
be surprised at what
you can change and learn.

A void repetitive negative
abuse within your
spiritual core; it can grow
like a fungus.

Chapter Seven

GINA

Gina was sixteen years old and lived in Wayne, PA. She had auburn hair and stood five feet seven. Her long soft shiny beautiful hair was the envy of her classmates, although Gina's body needed a little work. She also had a fairly large dark brown wart on her nose that detracted from her beauty. In spite of her challenges she felt confident, pretty, and cute. Some people felt sorry for Gina while others admired her.

At home, Gina endured a constant stream of demands from her mother. Her mother said, "Gina, Will you feed the baby? Gina, get dinner started, I have errands to run. Gina, Louie has a project due for the boy scouts, could you help him? Gina, no you can't go to the dance until the kitchen floor is scrubbed. You know the rule and by the way, your Dad and I are going out to dinner tomorrow. I expect you'll watch the baby. Gina, we can't afford the cost of you to get your license even though you are sixteen and are old enough. We need you at home." "Yes, Mama, yes Mama," said Gina. "I'll do it. Whatever! Maybe Ryan will call tonight! How I hate being a slave in this house!"

Besides Ryan on her mind, her studies were nonsense to her. She just about passed with a C+. Gina loved to read fashion magazines and think about Ryan. Ryan was the answer. If only she could have more time to spend with him. Ryan was a high school hallway patrol officer and he had a nice look about him that was neat and smart. At school, he always looked Gina's way. Ryan called and asked her for a date and Gina accepted.

One thing led to another. Ryan and Gina went steady for two years and got married right after Gina's high school graduation. Ryan was one year older than Gina and had joined the Marines. Gina wanted to get out of her house so bad, that she did not think twice about getting married to Ryan.

They had two daughters very quickly although loved the girls he secretly always wanted a boy. But it did not happen. Gina became a lonely service wife that stayed home to watch the children while Ryan worked crazy hours or so he said. Days went into years and years went into decades. Gina got extremely chubby and out of shape while Ryan stayed fit. Gina could not help that she was very resentful of him. She almost wished to be the slave of her mother again. Or was she a maid sort of and instead of her mother being the controller, it was her husband.

Life went on and Gina stayed married to Ryan in name only. She started going out without Ryan when her daughters got to be teenagers. Ryan and Gina led separate lives but lived as husband and wife in name only. Gina took a look at herself one day, and said, "How did life pass me by?" She got a divorce from Ryan and went to weight watchers. Gina also went to a dermatologist and had her wart on her nose removed along with her nose reconstructed. It was time to stop the excuses and start living. Gina got a job at a local doctor's office running the front office. This was the first time at age forty-five that Gina felt good about herself and what she was doing. Her daughters respected her for changing her life around physically and emotionally. Gina felt positive, happy, knowing she was finally being her true self.

PERSONAL NOTES

H eal your broken heart with warm memories.

E mbrace the moment as it will soon be a memory.

N otice when it is time to say "Goodbye."

R epair physical and emotional hardships with love.

I ncorporate love lessons with life lessons.

E voke positive thoughts through positive energy.

T reat yourself to education; you can do it.

T hink about the good in your life and get rid of negativity.

A ssure yourself that you are at the right moment at the right time.

Chapter Eight

HENRIETTA

"Henrietta, Henrietta, come out and play!" said Joey McGill. As Henrietta peeked outside her living room window, it was Joey as usual. Everyday Joey came to get her since they were four years old. Henrietta was turning seven and Joey turning eight. They were one year and a couple of days apart in age and lived in Rockville, MD.

They always talked, played games, argued, and discussed family matters. Joey's dad, a sailor from the Navy left them when his little brother was born. He left Joey's mom with five kids and no money. Henrietta's mom acted like a child herself and her dad was an alcoholic. He used to beat her, swear at her, and tell her she was a whore. She didn't even know what a whore was. Her mom just let the beatings happen as she was immature and afraid of confrontation. So the bond between Henri and Joey got stronger; and it was Henri and Joey day after day, year after year.

When Henri was eleven, Joey kissed her on her front porch and said to her, "Henrietta, will you be the mother of my children? I want you to be their mother." Well, Henri confused but proudly said, "Of course!" Henrietta was in love and so was Joey. It was the way it was supposed to be. Joey was going to high school next year. Life was glorious when they were together, but things changed as soon as Joey went to high school. He didn't want to talk to Henri anymore and when he did, it was all about the band, football, groups, and what not. One day Henri looked out of her window and saw Joey with other people. He said that they were his mother's friends' daughters, and that he had to be with them. They even went on vacation together and Joey enjoyed their friendship which helped make him more outgoing. He got so outgoing that he flirted with a neighbor named Teri down the street. One day Joey and Teri were holding hands and Joey never bothered with Henrietta ever again.

Henri went on her way the following year to a different high school than Joey and Joey was still being Mr. Social at his high school. Life for them was never again a pair and their relationship just dissolved without any words or contact.

One August day, Henri, in her mid-twenties, came out of her house in her wedding gown looking more beautiful than she ever did. Joey saw her, stood and just stared. A friend of Henri's pulled up with a sparkling white Camaro and Henri jumped in. She was driven away never to return to the old neighborhood again except to visit her mother on occasion.

Henri married Steve who was a lawyer and helped Henri go through college and then onto law school. She passed the bar exam and became a successful lawyer. Henri also stayed beautiful as she grew older. She was a happy wonderful wife, mother and lawyer. While Joey spent most of his life not sure of what he really wanted. Not sure of this and not sure of that. He had a psychological profile problem and often acted in plays to fulfill something in his life that was missing.

Twenty-five years have passed and Joey was fifty and Henrietta forty-nine years old. Henri's husband Steve passed away and Henri took take a higher paying position in Washington, DC. Both Joey and Henri commuted to their out of state jobs and both were settled in a lifestyle they were accustomed to. Thoughts lingered about not saying goodbye properly some forty years or so ago. Joey's mother saw Henri at a funeral a few months ago. Her eyes clouded up, she took Henri's hand, they hugged and as they were holding hands she said, "Henrietta, you look the same after all these years!" Henri replied, "Thank you for the delicious cake you used to bake. I really never forgot it and how kind you were to me and how you always shared your cake with me on the porch." Joey's mom just stood and stared holding onto Henri's hands and words could not explain what was said through her eyes. She then said, "Stop over for lunch, we'd love to see you." Joey's Mom and Henrietta both knew they would never see each other again and the parting glances were emotional. Time went on and Henri always wanted to stop over and pay Joey's Mom a visit, but something always held her back. It was that eleven-year-old year girl that got hurt and never really got over it! As her memory was recorded, "Henrietta, Henrietta, come out and play?"

Joey's mom passed away many years later and Henri went to the wake. Now Henri and Joey were close to sixty years old. Henri was, even at this age, beautiful and gracious in a new suit that she was wearing. Joey thanked her for coming, took her hand and said, "Oh, you are so beautiful but I put on a little weight. Do you have any children? Henri replied, "Yes, a boy and a girl." They held hands and stared at each other. Tears flooded both their eyes. For a fleeting second, a lifetime had not gone by but Joey and Henri were three and four again but knowingly that they will never see each other again.

PERSONAL NOTES

I mprove your knowledge of tanning and tattoos; is it right for your body?

N avigate your career to include your life's mission.

E xamine your ultimate reason for choosing someone or something; write it down. Reexamine this reason when circumstances change.

Z ooming through stages of life can bring positive and negative change; be careful about zooming!

Chapter Nine

INEZ

Inez was five feet tall, Spanish decent, thirty-four years old, and about a size four who lived in Bridgeport, CT. With dark reddish brown hair and freckles, she had a kind of a cute but messy look about her. She had an unusual mannerism with raising her eyebrows up and down as she spoke. She commuted to New York City from Connecticut for her job. Her job in the city was with a sports magazine focusing on motorcycle racing; she had the best job on the face of the earth, or so she thought. She spent fifteen days a month in Daytona Beach, FL and fifteen days in New York City while living with her husband in Connecticut. Life couldn't be better but deep down she was thought she was missing something.

Marital problems occurred with her husband Patrick. Patrick had a construction business and was content working with the guys, coming home to his beer, TV, and snacks. Inez got tired of this routine after four years of marriage. She and Patrick got divorced and she could not wait to be single again. Inez decided to move to Daytona Beach, FL.

She convinced her employer to switch her time at her job. She got them to say yes to working in Daytona

Beach permanently. Time was dragging for Inez as she counted down the days when she would officially move from Connecticut to Daytona Beach. Motorcycle racing and writing was her life! She would have been a motorcyclist had she been taller; now she opted for writing about all the races and meeting all those handsome drivers and in the sunshine and partying! But one thing held her captive – the more she bathed and played in the sun, the tanner she got. At first she thought she looked beautiful but the tanning got her older looking by the minute.

Inez was divorced and loved being single again. She dated men ten years younger than herself. She went to party after party. One day she even got a tattoo on her backside so she could show it off to whomever. Time went on and Inez woke up one morning and took a look at herself in the bright sunshine and started to cry. She arrived three years ago a beautiful thirty-eight year old women and now she thought she looked old. The more she looked at herself, the worse she looked. Was this life of tanning and partying really worth it? Also, she just couldn't keep up with all the new young writers coming into town and eyeing her job.

Inez went to a resume expert and got her resume redone. She started to apply for jobs at more conservative magazines. She got a call from a cooking magazine for an interview. "Well, that must be boring," she said to herself. She went on the interview anyway. They needed a person to write recipes, cook the item, shoot the pictures, and clean up. Would she be interested? Since that was her only call, she said, "Yes."

Inez started her new job on Monday and Tuesday fell in love with the design editor. He was a handsome mature man about forty-five years old. He asked her to marry him and told her that he got a job offer that he couldn't refuse in New York City. Would she go with him? Or would he give up the job offer to be her in Daytona Beach. Inez said yes to marriage and to moving to New York City. Even though she didn't ever want to go back to the east coast anymore, she did. Inez was emotional and a little confused about life and its complexity of changes. She learned not to suntan too as it has negative effects. In New York City, she ended up getting a position at a well-known publisher as an editor's assistant and hoped to be on her way to someday being an editor.

PERSONAL NOTES

J udge yourself not too hard; relax and have fun.

E ndure the process of chance; you may be lucky!

S poil yourself once in awhile; remember it with a smile.

S ing if you can and if you can't, try anyways. Same thing with spelling, if you can't spell, get a dictionary. Just don't say, "I can't."

I mprove your game in which you are interested; if you don't have a game learn one. It might take you on an unforgettable journey.

E mpower yourself and other to make time for pleasures!

Chapter Ten

JESSIE

Jesse seemed to always have the answer. She watched all the game shows and dreamt of being a contestant. She was thirty-four years old and lived in a small town called Surprise, AZ. She had a dream of fame and fortune. Jesse lived by herself in a small apartment and cared for her pet cat named Candy.

One day there was an advertisement to be a contestant on the Wheel of Fortune. Jesse sent in the required information and six months later the Wheel of Fortune contestant recruiter called her. Jesse was asked a few questions like any game question and that was that. Days went by and she never heard anything again. Until one day early in May the phone rang and it was a Wheel of Fortune scheduler for the game. She was asked to participate! Jesse was so excited especially since she would be going to New York City for the game. Jesse had never been out of Arizona, nevertheless, a big city like New York. As news travels fast, her friends were mighty jealous and Jesse was popular. The date was set for filming in November. The date seemed far away at first, but the day came quicker than she thought. Jesse needed winter clothes of which she never wore. She got a catalog and ordered a winter coat, gloves, scarf, and a hat.

The plane ticket to LaGuardia Airport was in her hand and off she went to the big city. Jesse arrived at LaGuardia Airport one day before the show and was planning to stay a week. The studio booked her a room at the Waldorf Astoria on Park Avenue. Jesse walked in the foyer and saw beautiful crystal chandeliers, rich fancy wood moldings surrounded by a quaint setting with accents of marble. She thought she died and went to heaven! The doormen were richly clad in their winter capes and hats. Limousines were parked everywhere. Jesse was escorted to her room to be pleasantly surprised to find a dozen red roses from NBC Studios.

Well, the morning soon arrived and a limo was parked out front waiting for Jesse. She got in and went to the taping of the Wheel of Fortune. She was very nervous as she had been studying for over six months and everyone from Surprise, Arizona was watching her. As the day turned out, Jesse was waiting to solve the puzzle to the grand prize for $50,000.00 cash and a new BMW convertible. Her hands were sweating and her heart was going so fast she blurted out an answer! What seemed like forever but was only seconds, she won the prizes!

In tears, and no one there with her, she seemed frozen in her movements!

Well, after the show she got a tour of NBC Studios and dinner at The View restaurant which revolves while viewing scenic Manhattan. This turned out to be some evening as it continued to be exciting with the tree lighting ceremony at Rockefeller Center. People were pouring in from everywhere. Jesse saw the beautiful tree at Rockefeller Center get lit. She then walked down Park Avenue and window-shopped. She stayed in New York City for three more days site seeing. She saw the Statue of

Liberty, St. Patrick's Cathedral, Ellis Island, China town, Wall Street and course, Central Park.

Tears flooded Jesse's eyes when the limo took her to LaGuardia to go back to Surprise, Arizona. For this week, she truly was like Cinderella! This was undoubtedly a memorable event in her life that she would never forget.

Jesse grew old some forty years later and she revisits the week in the "Big Apple" to anyone that will listen. As she tells her story, Cinderella comes back to life one more time with a twinkle in her eyes that has never dimmed!

PERSONAL NOTES

K eep what is close to your heart close; but reevaluate it every so often.

E ntertain thoughts of happiness.

L augh during stressful moments to ease tension; it may break the tension.

L oafing someone may turn to loving someone.

Y earning for connectivity in your life is a positive flow of energy; serendipity happens with no explanation, enjoy the moment!

Chapter Eleven

KELLY

Strictly business and only business was Kelly's motto. Get them before they get you. Being a trader at the NYSE at twenty-seven was a tough game to play. She drinks her coffee black, works out at the gym, does karate, and lives in Manhattan. Kelly grew up in Brooklyn and hung out with the crowd from the street. She never took drugs and the street people knew her since she was just a kid. They said, "This is the kid who is going to make money someday and show all of them up!"

Kelly's parents were poor and never had the money to send her to college. She was smart enough to fill out the financial aid forms herself and got accepted into New York University (NYU). She got a degree in Finance. It was her Brooklyn accent and her little tough aggressiveness that got her an assistant trader position. Within six months, she took the Series 7 and 55 tests and she passed. The next year Kelly earned $250,000 and enjoyed the lifestyle that it brought.

Kelly got married to Mark who was a handsome would-be actor. Fortunately Kelly brought in enough money to support them, their Park Avenue apartment, the cleaning service, the cook, and the driver. However, after a hectic and exciting morning of trading, Kelly got ill. A headache and nausea overwhelmed her and she headed home early. When she arrived at the apartment at an unexpected time, she heard laughing, chatter, and music coming from her apartment.

Kelly's knees turned into jelly and opened the door. He husband Mark was kissing another women and had not noticed her arrival. Kelly said, "How do you dare?" The woman and Mark flung apart but the scene was like a horror film! Kelly's headache and nausea got worse and she fainted. When she woke up in her bed, she found a note from Mark. "Dear Kelly, I am sorry for hurting you but I just don't love you anymore and I am leaving you."

Days went by and Kelly's nausea never went away. She found out that she was pregnant with Mark's child. "Oh, no!' she said and cried herself to sleep. Kelly continued to work and had a baby boy named Michael. He looked like Mark in every way; even his grin looked like Michael as he was about to get into mischief.

One day Kelly took Michael who was now sixteen years old to a Broadway play. Michael turned into a tall handsome young man with dark wavy hair like his father. He was happy to see the play as it was opening night. The actors were in the foyer greeting the press and taking publicity photos. A middle-aged man with silver gray hair at his temples turned around so the camera can get a better shot. He accidentally bumped into Michael. He was about to say excuse me when the actor looked at Kelly and Michael! Standing before him was the most beautiful woman in his life that he secretly never got over and this young man that looked like he did when he was a teenager! Mark's eyes flooded with tears and said to Kelly, "Kelly, I never stopped loving you after all these years! And may I be introduced to your date?" Kelly said,

"Mark, this is Michael, your son. I did not know you were still an actor and I did not bring him here on purpose." A heavily made-up blond lady rudely interrupted them and said, "Mark honey, our guests are waiting honey bunch." Mark's eyes could not help staring at Kelly and Michael and then was pulled to a group of people waiting for him.

Michael said, "You never told me I looked just like him!" Kelly said, "I just couldn't, he hurt me too much and I never got over it." Kelly and Michael went into the theater to see a performance of a lifetime. Mark got a standing ovation and with his hands up tried to stop everyone from clapping. He was in tears with the spotlight on him. He told the camera crew to focus on Kelly and Michael. He then said, "I dedicate this performance to my dear wife Kelly and son Michael." He walked out to them with the spotlight following him, they cried and hugged, and *three became one.*

PERSONAL NOTES

L ove your work; the rest will follow.

O bey your limitations; honor your strengths.

R ead every day to keep the channel of knowledge flowing.

I nstill good thoughts about your present day and your future.

Chapter Twelve

LORI

Lori started her every day with a prayer. She was twenty-two years old just yesterday and was wondering what she was going to do with her life. She lived in Denver, CO. She graduated college with honors with a major in General Studies a couple of months ago. She decided to take a break and see what would happen as she had no particular interest in anything special.

One day she was cleaning her room and found a note on her nightstand. The bright yellow paper note was typed and said, "Believe in yourself and the world is Yours." She asked her mother if she did it and her mother said, "No." Her father and brother also said, "No." The only living thing that she had left was Buster, the family dog. She was sure Buster did not do it as he couldn't type. Interesting! Well, oddly enough Lori started thinking about the note. Nothing ever interested her or made her feel wow! "Believe in yourself and the World is Yours!"

Lori decided to call her friend Jody and chat with her on the phone. She wanted to run this by Jody. Jody said, "Well, at least it is a positive note!"

A week went by and another note appeared on the nightstand. This note read, "To thy own self be true!" The note was typed again on the bright yellow paper. She asked her family if someone was doing this and no one admitted to this.

The third week came and Lori started thinking about what she wanted to be. She now thought seriously about becoming a doctor and something drove her into thinking about clinical research. She was an honor student in college but always was bored. You know, boredom being called the ho-hum syndrome. Lori decided to call her own physician to ask for a recommendation on maybe becoming a doctor. Her doctor said that Yale University Medical School was always looking for candidates especially young people that were as bright as she was. She then called the admissions office at Yale and they told her she would have to apply and that she would need three recommendations. Dr. George, her physician, Professor Dudley, her college chemistry professor, and her neighbor, Shelly Morton, who had known Lori for her whole life, were asked to write recommendations for her.

Another week went by and another note appeared. This one said, "Find your mission in life and you will never be lonely and your work will make mankind a better place." Strange note but again the notes got Lori thinking. Then one day the mail came and it was Yale University Medical School saying that she was accepted. One event led to another and another. She then enrolled and attended medical school for six years. When Lori finished medical school she continued doing research with the hope of developing a cure for cancer.

Months went by and then Lori's mother got diagnosed with cancer of the uterus and eventually died. Lori, a doctor herself, could not save her life. As life would have it, Lori was helping her father by cleaning out some of her mother's private things in her "special box" as she used to call it. Lori opened the box and found old pictures of friends, old jewelry, cards from friends, and on the bottom of the box was a stack of yellow note cards. They were identical to the notes Lori had found on her nightstand. It was her Mom that typed the notes to encourage Lori to find herself especially since the note on the top of the pile said, "Cancer – Malignant." She wanted Lori to find her mission in her own way as her life would be ending and she knew all along that Lori had the ability to be a fine research physician and hopefully save other lives.

PERSONAL NOTES

M ake music not noise.

E njoy life's fruit; it brings
sweetness to our day.

T ry to find your rhythm in life
and follow its course.

T reat yourself to food and
drink at festivals; listen to the
music in your heart and smile.

Y our spirit is the breadth of life
here on earth to remind us
how we are all connected to
the universe.

Chapter Thirteen

METTY

Metty is the short version of her name; she is otherwise known as Methuselah by the townspeople in the mainland of Hawaii. Her age was unknown, and she has never cut her hair which was symbolic of her power. She gave Hawaiian folk dance lessons forever it seems. Even some grandmothers had studied with her. "The Teacher, The Dancer, The Music Maker." She was a symbol of the magic of Hawaiian folklore.

Many people thought that she was an eccentric individual; but others regarded her as precious. Metty went about her business of teaching every day. It is what she has known her entire life. Metty doesn't remember when she learned to dance and chant. She always knew so it seemed.

One day Metty was at a Hawaiian festival and it was her turn to chant and play along with two of her students. She was appropriately decorated in her leaf skirt and fresh flower lei. She started drumming and chanting. The students danced and the audience chanted along with her. All of a sudden, clouds appeared in a bright sunny sky. Thunder rolled in and lightening filled the sky. The crowd thinned out and only a few of the regulars stayed behind.

Metty continued her drumming and chanting along with her students who were still dancing and drumming in a methodical rhythm. Lightening appeared again and hit a tree not too far from what was left of the crowd. The rest of the townspeople left the festival and Metty and her student dancers were the only ones still in attendance.

They did not stop chanting, singing, dancing, and drumming. It was as if they got empowered by the energy of the lightening. Soon the clouds disappeared as if it were magic. The bright blue sky of Hawaii appeared and the sun seemed to be brighter than ever. A voice came out of nowhere and said, "Metty, your spirit will always be protected from harms way because you have the spirit of the universe. Your mother is with me now and she still watches over you. You are a special person of nature to help people understand the beauty of dance and song. I came to you today because it is the feast of the "Wind" and you will always be in my heart and be watched over. Your students will continue your work and they too will commission others to be the water carrier of dance and song."

Metty and her students looked around and saw no one. The song and dance had ended and they looked at the beautiful table of fresh fruit and special teas and decided that they would partake of what was left of the festival. They ate and drank tea and decided to head back home. No one spoke of the voice they all heard and it appeared that no one ever did. They kept it to themselves. They were moments to be treasured and to be left unspoken.

PERSONAL NOTES

N ever give up; project positive thoughts and they will return to you.

I nspire others with enthusiastic perseverance.

N eed love; give love..

A llow happiness and peace to come to you.

Chapter Fourteen

NINA

Nina was a young lady that was twenty years old and lived in Port St. Lucy, FL. She was about five feet four with long dark wavy hair.

Nina remembered falling in love with Martin when she met him that spring. It was love at first sight. Martin's ship came in off the Gulf of Mexico and Nina was a baker's daughter who would bring bread to the gathering at the village's café inn at the dock. Martin and Nina hit it off and before you know it, love was in the air. When Nina woke up the next morning, there was a note on her pillow saying, "Nina, I will love you forever and I want you to have my gold medal of St. Martin that my father had given to me. The medal was engraved, "*To Martin, May God keep you safe and out of harms way, love Dad.*" "It is the only possession that I have of value and I want you to keep it. My shipmates need me and the sea is calling," love Martin.

Tears flooded up in Nina's eyes and at that very moment, she knew that she would never see Martin again. He loved the adventure of the sea and all of its glory. Days turned into months and Nina gave birth to Martin's child. She named him, "Jacque." On Jacque's Baptism, Nina gave Jacque his father's gold medal. He was a charming little boy and looked just like his father, Martin. He had a twinkle in his eyes that would charm anyone, especially if wrongdoing was done.

When Jacque grew up, he used to deliver the bread from the bakery for Nina, as she now was the owner of the bakery. Nina's specialty was her father's olive bread. This was a recipe that was in the family for years and was never written down.

One day Jacque who was about thirteen years old, took his dingy a little too far in the ocean. The sea was choppy and fog started setting in. Nina started wondering why Jacque wasn't home for dinner. She went to the dock and asked his friends if they had seen him. No one had seen him except in the early afternoon when he took the dingy out. Nina got nervous and searched the gulf for a week to follow. Jacque was never found.

It had been the townspeople's gossip that Nina, the baker, baked bread every day to bring it to the village café herself everyday in hope of seeing a new ship come in. She waited and hoped for the day when Jacque would come home. She prayed to St. Martin for the safety of her son even though the coast rescue team had deemed him dead.

Over twenty years have gone by and Nina was now close to sixty years old with gray hair. She still baked bread every day and brought it to the village café dock. Some people say she has gotten hard with age and others say she still waits and hopes for her son's return.

One stormy August night a ship came in with a bunch of sailors. Nina brought over her olive bread as it was all she had left in the bakery. The sailors were happy to be fed and to have a warm fire in the stone fireplace. Someone played the harmonica while another sailor quietly played his guitar. Some of the people from town brought over left-over food from their night's dinner and a party was being had by all.

Nina did not leave the café that night as she normally would have done. Since the storm was still unsettled, she thought that she should have a glass of wine and enjoy the music. The sailor's group leader was young handsome man that had a twinkle in his eyes and knew the sea. It was his ship so she gathered. Something about him intrigued Nina; it was the twinkle in his eyes and the sense of adventure of the sea.

Nina made an excuse to talk to him. Why would he want to talk to an old woman? But she pursued. She made her way through the crowd and asked him if he had some of the bread. It was as if they had always known each other. Nina was so happy that she could almost see her son in this young man! He responded that he liked the olive bread very much and it tasted like something familiar that he might have had before. Nina was getting very old in years and what did she know? Had the years and her life just gotten the best of her? Nina asked the young sailor captain about his background and he said, "My love has always been the sea and that is my family." Nina and the young sailor talked for hours and then she headed home. The sailors took rooms at the sea's inn nearby. The next day they were boarded the ship and decided to leave.

Like clockwork, Nina delivered her bread to the café inn and said that she would help clean the inn as the sailors left it untidy. Nina went from room to room and in the fourth room she found something very interesting. On the sheet near the pillow, there laid a gold medal of St. Martin and it was inscribed, *"To Martin, May God keep you safe and out of harms way, love Dad."* Tears flooded Nina's eyes! Nina said, "Jacque?" She ran to see if she could see if the ship had left and as she got to the pier, the ship sailed into the blue sky of the Gulf of Mexico. Nina cried and cried but they were tears of joy, "Jacque was alive and well!"

PERSONAL NOTES

O ffer your thoughts when asked.

R eward yourself by dressing up.

Y ell at yourself when you goof up; then learn the lesson and move on.

E ntertain thoughts of your perfect mission.

L ink happiness with challenges learned and reward yourself.

L ike yourself from the inside out.

A fford opportunities to others if you can.

Chapter Fifteen

ORYELLA

Oryella was a fashion designer who thought she knew everything. She was successful by the age of thirty years old and she had the world at her fingertips. She was five feet ten and looked like a model and she lived in Los Angeles, CA; she was now forty-one years old. Fashion was her life and that was about all, or was it? Patterns, styles, what was in, what was out. That was Oryella's life so it seemed. Life got so complicated with styles and trends that Oryella did not know if she wanted to stay in the business at age forty-one. "Shall I continue or shall I find a safe harbor for my talents? I can write for a magazine, newsletter or get a job anywhere; just as long as it is anywhere but not in the fashion business."

Fashions by Oryella were fashions that everyone knew. Oddly enough, Oryella wanted to out of the business so it seemed. Life as a fashion designer was not easy; she flew back and forth from California to London, Rome, Paris, and New York. The intense amount of traveling was enough to keep up with. Oryella had a goal in life to create fashion elements to encourage all ages to be beautiful. Her fashions were for women who wanted to be in professional careers and for women who just wanted to be fashionable.

Sometimes a person has to feel what they want to be. Oryella created a contest. The contest was, "Create a suitable wardrobe for a woman 27 – 37 years old to be what they wanted to be. This was a challenge especially for a fashion designer who ended up wanting everyone to look like they were wearing a cookie cutter mold.

Well, the contest was open and 1,100 individuals entered. The judging was not easy. The winner was a young mother who had no money but came up with the "Blue Effort."

The "Blue Effort" was as follows:
Be who you are.
Love others as yourself.
Understand your co-workers and colleague.
Everyone is special.

Every person has a chance.
Find who you are.
Forgive all that you are not.
Organize what you can and leave the rest.
Repair old garments, they tell their own story.
Time is of the essence; don't waste what you may not have.

The "Blue Effort" was essentially everything every woman needed to be successful along with a great fashion sense of style. Oryella congratulated the winner of the contest and gave her the prize of $10,000.00 and a job in fashion. Oryella decided to take the methodology of the "Blue Effort" seriously into her own life and decided it was time to explore a new career possibly in teaching fashion design.

PERSONAL NOTES

P repare yourself for the unexpected but don't live in the
future.

A llow yourself to live in the
present moment; go ahead,
take a deep breath and forget
yesterday.

O wn your own feelings; when
love happens let it and smile;
when grief happens let it and
cry. Love is eternal.

Chapter Sixteen

PAO

Pao was an Indian Chief's wife who was about fifty years old who lived in White Bear Lake, MN. She had problems with the other squaws in the tribe. They liked to flirt with her husband Chief Blue Bird. Her husband, Chief Blue Bird enjoyed the attention.

One day Pao said, "This is it! I am not going to take it anymore!" She packed up her bags and left for the ocean with just enough fruit, berries, and nuts for a week. Pao thought that she would be at the ocean in a week. She would settle there and set up her own tent. Pao made it to the ocean in four days. The ocean was beautiful as was the pure white sand warm from the sun beating down on it.

Soon it became evening and Pao set up her tent. She started gathering wood for a fire to keep her warm. This is nice, "She said to herself! No one around and it was peaceful and quiet".

A noise sounded into the night. Someone was here! There were gunshots and the sound was getting closer! Pao stayed still in the tent and did not move. Even her breath seemed like too much noise!

Pao heard men's voices! They almost sounded familiar! One of which called out her name. It was Chief Blue Bird. He came with some other men looking for her. Pao decided to come out of the tent to confront the group. Chief Blue Bird saw Pao and came running. "Pao, I am so worried about you, why did you leave?" Pao crumbled to the ground speechless. Weak from the journey and very nervous, she trembled and started to cry. Chief Blue Bird summonsed the four others in his group and told them to leave two horses and go back to the village and tribe.

Chief Blue Bird said again, "Pao oh Pao, why did you leave?" Pao answered, "I felt that all you ever wanted was the attention from all the other women in the tribe. I felt useless and unhappy." Well, Chief Blue Bird said, "No Pao, the others try to show off. I will not let them ever take my attention from you ever again. Will you come back with me?" Pao looked at the ocean and thought, "Let's spend the night and talk in the morning."

One day followed the next and one week had passed. Pao and Blue Bird decided to build a small cabin on the ocean. Blue Bird had forgotten about the beauty of the sun, wind, sky, and ocean. He had gotten all caught up with the power of being the chief. Blue Bird revisited the elements of life all over again as if it were a magical journey.

Pao was glad to have her husband back. They took walks, swam in the ocean, picked fruit, berries, and nuts, and gathered wood for their evening fires. Then one day someone from the tribe came to visit. He said that trouble was brewing back home amongst the tribe. The young rebels of the tribe wanted to take over because Chief Blue Bird was not there.

The morning came and without a note or anything, Blue Bird was gone and so was the other tribe member. Pao knew his tribe was calling him. He didn't even say goodbye.

Two weeks past and another tribe member came to visit Pao. He said, "I am the bearer of sad news." Pao's eyes filled with tears. She almost didn't want to hear the rest. She knew. The message was that Chief Blue Bird tried to stop a fight and was shot in the heart and killed instantly. Pao told him to leave and that she would not be going back.

Pao cried and cried. The ocean would sing a song of peace to help her stop crying. The wind would kick up to refresh her face and the sun warmed her back. It was said that passers-by would often see an Indian woman walking by the ocean and calling Blue Bird's name. Eventually, Pao got old and died. There were tales that a woman's footprints could be found in the sand at Ocean Hill and it was said that they were the footprints of the spirit of Pao still looking for her husband Blue Bird.

PERSONAL NOTES

Q uench even the slightest thought of taking something that is not yours.

U nearth your own talents and your riches will be yours.

I magine having success and it will come to you.

N egotiate clear agreements with others and put it in writing so no one is disappointed.

C ease to hold grudges, forgive and move on.

Y earn for a rich life in whatever you like and the positive force will pave your future.

Chapter Seventeen

QUINCY

Quincy McLaughlin was a bright young woman who was thirty-two years old and lived in Boston, MA. Quincy, graduated law school with the status of Magna Cum Laude that she could not get out of her head. Attorney at Law was a dream and now it was real. Quincy worked hard for her degree and receiving honors was especially nice.

Quincy had a job already lined up at the Superior Court, in Massachusetts. It just so happened that when Quincy sent in her resume, a job just opened due to one of Boston's finest attorneys who had retired. Being that Quincy was a minority and a woman, she quickly engaged an interview. Subsequently, Quincy got the job. As her husband Jacob would say, "Don't cross Quincy if you can help it."

The biggest trial that was coming up was Joan Hyden vs. Jonathan and Arlene Hyden. It was a case that was nationwide. Quincy knew she had a challenge and she was preparing for it.

The case history was about a child who was an actress and about twenty-one years old. Her parents spent her gross income to lead the so-called good life. It was when

Quincy said, "I pronounce the defendant, "Guilty as charged." The verdict was to make the plaintiff whole, and all of the gross income of Joan Hyden shall be deemed as her sole income and hers for every day that she worked. It was her sole income not to be spent otherwise.

Joan was happy although that meant her parents would have to pay for everything they had spent while she did her soap career. Quincy was not sure how the public would take her first case. She was definitely sure that Joan earned all of this money and therefore, should have receipt of it in her bank account.

The parents had too many excuses that were not too tangible on why they spent her money. Joan deserved more. Quincy knew that she had done the right thing and felt fine until she received a phone call from Joan's mother. Her mother said that Joan decided to buy a home for herself and one for her parents. She just wanted them to learn that it was not their money to take. She forgave them and would give them a home after they paid her back.

Sometimes it happens in life that there are lessons to be learned and that was one of them. This lesson was not spending someone else's money. However, love prevails and Joan forgave them.

As for Quincy, the case was perfect for her. She got noticed and her career got off to a booming start. All of those years of law school paid off and she was able to say in a confident tone, "Case Dismissed."

PERSONAL NOTES

R eexamine your life's goals every so often and see where it takes you.

I ncur your own strength to follow your heart.

S avor time spent with a special person.

A scertain if you love someone; then realize that person is human and can make mistakes. This is a reminder that we are not perfect either.

Chapter Eighteen

RISA

Risa Marie Brockman was a registered nurse for five years. She was about thirty years old and lived in Kansas City, MO. Since Risa was five years old, all she ever wanted to be was a nurse. Risa was fortunate and smart enough to receive a four-year Bachelor of Science scholarship in nursing from her Kansas City, MO high school.

Onward to her career in medicine, her turmoil began when she realized that she should have been a doctor. But as life would have it, she did not have the money for college nevertheless, medical school. Nursing was quite rewarding to Risa. She was a specialist in trauma therapy. Risa assisted the physician when a patient experienced trauma.

Risa also assisted in routine physical analysis and then onto physiotherapy. She loved her job and enjoyed helping people although the thought always bothered her that should have been a doctor.

One day a man came into the hospital. He appeared to be about her age. He was in a bad car accident and bleeding everywhere. He was a racecar driver and lost a race to someone who cheated during the race. He had labored his time and spent all of his money to invest in this car race. However, someone on the sidelines shot his tires and he was doomed. The car smashed into the sidelines and flipped over. Risa took his personal information and noticed that he was not married. No other relative except his mother. His name was Justin.

Risa fell in love with Justin on the spot. Justin needed physiotherapy. Risa challenged herself, had she been his physician, would falling in love with a patient be proper? She questioned herself. Risa assisted Justin in therapy and he finally asked her on a date. Risa accepted the date and felt love in the air. Risa had marriage in her heart but didn't know if Justin did.

Risa then questioned herself, "If she had been a physician, something she always wanted, would she had fallen in love with Justin? Justin asked Risa to marry him two years later and he now changed his career to programming. The question about Risa becoming a doctor was over. She was glad to be a nurse and now she questions whether being a doctor would have been right for her as life with Justin is ever so happy.

PERSONAL NOTES

S hare your dreams and life's work with others.

E mbrace your loved ones, time is but a fleeting moment and soon becomes yesterday.

R ethink your goals and needs at different stages of your life.

E conomize where you can so financial goals don't have to direct your life's goals.

N esting with children is rich and valuable and never forgotten.

A ssociate yourself with others and share time.

Chapter Nineteen

SERENA

Serena Randolph was thirty-seven years old, five feet four, had blond hair, and lived in Carson City, NV. She was CEO of her own start-up company having invented a widget that attached buttons to fabric. It was a plastic device that shot a piece of plastic in a fabric and you would attach your button onto it. Serena had a company of twenty-five employees. She loved her career and believed nothing would stop her long hours and commitment to her company of twenty-five employees.

Serena's husband of two years, Daniel, was equally busy as the disk jockey at the local radio station. His work hours were long and his schedule constantly changing. Serena felt ill, they assumed it was the flue. But her nausea and exhaustion didn't go away. After numerous trips to the doctor and a full battery of tests, she was shocked to learn that she was pregnant. Serena had a healthy pregnancy and delivered baby twins one month early. Serena had a C-section and she and the babies were fine. She named the babies Bridget and Bryce. As time went on, Serena returned to work and found her days in turmoil. She then hired a nanny to watch and care for the twins.

Serena found out that she did not have any time for herself nevertheless with her husband.

Daniel tried to help out as best as he could but found his work hours to be long and tiresome. He worked various shifts and could not be counted on to take care of the babies at any specific time. Daniel had a beautiful deep voice and when he laughed, he sounded like Santa Claus. He loved being a DJ and going to community events on behalf of the station.

Serena came to the conclusion that she would quite her job, sell her business, and end her career as entrepreneur and businesswoman. She wanted to become a full-time mom. Daniel, who was very supportive, said that he thought that although they would suffer financially, as a family, they would enhance being a family unit and that they would live with it. Serena stayed at home to care for Bridget and Bryce. Serena would often play the radio for the twins to listen to their father on the radio. Although he couldn't be there in person, they listened to him and often would dedicate special messages to them. The children enjoyed being with Serena at home and consequently, this brought peace and order into their lives along with a healthy lifestyle.

PERSONAL NOTES

T ransmit positive energy and it will return to you.

H asten your mental and physical actions in time of danger.

E voke spirit to guide you in times of need.

R espect that others may be igno-rant and have not known love.

E ntreat respect and peace.

S peculate that your intuition will guide you through difficult situations.

A ccept the fact that others may not know what they are doing or why.

Chapter Twenty

THERESA

Theresa Shanahan was her name and she was the best fifth grade math teacher ever on the face of the earth…so she thought anyway, in the Bronx, NY. Theresa was twenty-eight years old and loved to teach, however guns became more prevalent and she became more hesitant. Did she pick the right career?

Theresa taught fifth grade children for five years and loved her career until guns came into the picture. She was a mere five feet and one inch and one hundred fifteen pounds. The rule on bringing guns to school was "Don't do it." The metal detector machine was broken and there were no funds to get it repaired. One day a student named Sissy brought a gun in her book bag. Theresa had no idea that there was a gun in the classroom. She finished with the math lesson for the day and much to her surprise Sissy started yelling at Tim.

Tim and Sissy were homework pals. Tim liked English and Sissy liked math. They were inseparable friends. Sissy was angry with Tim about helping another student named Judy out with her homework. Sissy approached him with her gun. She was going to shoot him if he did not obey her commands. Sissy went on to ask Tim to empty out his pockets for money. Well, Tim was hesitant but he did what he was asked. Sissy controlled the gun and it was up to Theresa to control the situation. Theresa firmly looked at Sissy in the eyes and asked, "Sissy, put the gun down, now!" Sissy looked at Theresa and was astounded! No one ever talked to her like that!

Sissy put the gun down and said that she was sorry and not sure why she even had a gun. Sissy went and hugged Theresa and said, "Thank you for drawing the line between good and bad. Sometimes I am not quite sure about either of them! I take care of my brothers and sisters at home and I am like their mother. My own mother has problems and she doesn't feel good all of the time." Theresa knew that Sissy and other children in her class had unbalanced home lives and knew that it was not easy to balance the problems at home and go to school.

Well, Theresa looked at the clock and it was five o'clock and thought that she should go home. It was quite a day! Theresa drove home to think, my oh, my, the role of a teacher is changing and ever so predominantly as one as "Mediator."

PERSONAL NOTES

U nlock your potential when life sends you on a detour; it may be for a reason.

R ecover from a set-back and reflect on your journey.

S peculate on positive affirmations to help you through difficult times.

U tilize your own assets to support yourself.

L iberate yourself from negative thought patterns.

A ccept lovely surprises with grace!

Chapter Twenty-One

URSULA

Ursula Krafitz was a fitness trainer at a gym in Stamford, Connecticut. She was forty-one years old and had been exercising for about twenty years. Ursula loved to teach aerobic classes and exercise too. She knew that she was helping people get physically fit and she felt good about it too. However, one day as she was leaving the gym, she slipped on a piece of ice. She fell and injured her back. She was out of work and had little or no money to pay for medical bills, as she did not carry medical insurance. Ursula was out of work and did not know when she was going back if ever. What would she do to support herself?

Ursula applied at a computer technology firm to be a secretary. She got the job but she was bored compared to her classes at the gym. Although Ursula was happy to support herself, she longed to back at the gym. She was healing but still needed to get more flexible and stronger before trying to be a trainer again. She met Kyle Garbien, Vice President of Technology, and he asked her to go on a date. She hesitated. She needed this job to support herself, as she did not know if she would ever be able to teach aerobics ever again. She did not go on the date but did meet him in the cafeteria at lunch occasionally. Kyle was smart and nice, but she thought he may be too bright for her.

One day Kyle met Ursula outside in the parking lot and gave her a bouquet of flowers. She said, "Thank you very much, these are beautiful!" Kyle said that he was going on a business trip to Aspen, Colorado and won't be around for two weeks. He was using some vacation time at work as well.

Well, two long weeks went by and Kyle came back. He stopped by Ursula's cubical and said that he had a surprise for her. He gave her a miniature wooden chalet ornament. Kyle told Ursula to open the door and she did. She saw a beautiful diamond ring. He looked at Ursula and said, "Will you marry me?" Tears swelled up in Ursula's eyes and said, "Yes!" The chalet ornament was a miniature duplicate of the home Kyle had just purchased. Ursula and Kyle got married one month later at a small chapel in Aspen with close friends that joined them.

Kyle relocated his office to his home studio in the south end of the Aspen chalet. Ursula went back to being an exercise instructor at the nearby ski lodge. If Ursula had not fallen on the ice that one cold December night and got injured, she would not have gotten the job at the technology company and met Kyle. Even though life has its challenges, there are reasons why we may take a special turn sometimes.

PERSONAL NOTES

*V*acate quickly when danger arrives.

*I*nvoke others to assist especially when they have the knowledge and the skills.

*C*ease to dwell on something that is ruined; move on.

*T*each children by good example.

*O*ffer a lending hand especially when disaster strikes.

*R*escue animals in danger.

*I*nclude and involve family members to help out.

*A*ttain your family's energy when needed.

Chapter Twenty-Two

VICTORIA

Victoria Browning was a young lady around thirty-two years old with light brown curly long hair who lived in Encinitas, CA. Victoria Browning gave birth to a boy named James on September 2nd and a year later a girl on September 7th named Janis. Her children were a joy to be around and just good kids and loved to play with their precious fur ball cat named Chilly. Vickie's husband Ken was happy to have two healthy children and a charming beautiful wife.

There were days of diapers, tricycles, colds and measles, but Vickie took care of those children. They lived in a country suburb and enjoyed the birds singing, trees swaying in the wind in the privacy of their yard. Until one day, an unexpected hurricane came to visit and wrecked their home. Fortunately, Vickie had the children at preschool at the time and she was at the grocery store. Vickie felt the forceful winds all around her; she frantically dropped her items and left the store to drive to the preschool. When she got there, the children were already put in a safety zone in the basement. It was a major task but Vickie found James and Janis together holding onto each other. With tears in her eyes, she saw them huddled together in a corner. When they saw her, they screamed, "Mommy!" Well, Vicki grabbed them frantically and started trembling. Her babies were okay! Other moms came to the preschool to get their children and they all felt the uncertain sense of danger. Soon the town's whistle had blown and they knew that the danger had passed.

Vickie, James, and Janis left to go home. The hurricane has passed and all that was left was some fine drizzling rain. When they reached home, they found that their house was demolished. Vickie's husband Ken was away on business and she felt useless at this point. The children wanted to look for their cat. Vickie did not want them in the ruins, as they may get hurt. Vickie called Ken on her cell phone and told him what happened. Ken said that he would catch the next flight home and make arrangements at the nearest hotel that was available and safe for the night.

However, the children and Vickie were still distraught over their missing kitten Chilly. Chilly was black and white with long fluffy fur and she was the children's best friend. Chilly was nowhere to be found. Vickie brought the children to the hotel and soon Ken arrived. He always had his mind together even though disaster stroke, he stayed calm and was already taking action by calling the insurance company.

The night was silent and the morning arrived with beautiful sunshine and a stillness that was quite prevalent. Ken, Vickie, James, and Janis arrived at what was left of their home. Police cars and fire trucks swarmed the street and it was hard to focus on what was next step to be done. James and Janis kept looking for Chilly. No Chilly to be found and the whole family started crying.

Ken told Vickie and the children to get into the car because they were in the way of the trucks and service people. All of a sudden a board from the garage moved and something was frantically crying. Vickie and the children ran to the board and Vickie pulled it up. Under the wreckage was a hurt Chilly that was crying, shaking and screaming frantically! She couldn't walk and was very scared. Well, the children hugged and kissed Chilly and the family went to the Dr. Dooley's office with her. Dr. Dooley said that she had a broken leg and a fractured rib cage but she will be okay. That night the whole exhausted family slept at the hotel with Chilly in their bed. She needed lots of care. The most important thing Vickie and her family learned was that it wasn't what you have in life but it is who you love that is important.

PERSONAL NOTES

*W*eave your life's work with
passion, creativity, and purity.

I nnovate new ideas to your
creative sense.

N ourish yourself to connect
with your intuition.

N udge the urge today to
expand your ambitions, "Can
you create something to enter
this contest? i.e. write a poem,
or essay, paint something,
build or cook something?

I llustrate your needs with
projected outcomes; see your
choices.

E radicate negative thoughts
with an "I can do or can be
attitude."

Chapter Twenty-Three

WINNIE

Winnie was an average size individual with short wispy black hair that was forty-three years old. She lived in Boston, MA in an apartment near the water.

Winnie was a cartoonist. She had a spot in the Boston Globe for her Sunday cartoon named "Woody and the Gang" and she was making a living as such.

Winnie decided to change her direction one day and drew a scene from a neighboring waterfall. She had a lovely day and painted the picture. There was a contest for local artists so she applied and registered her painting. Winnie won the contest and a five hundred dollar prize.

Turmoil inside of her got ignited, as she loved to paint natural woodland scenes; she really made her living as a cartoonist as it more than adequately paid her bills. She loved to draw even when she was a child. So Winnie took it upon herself to continue with the cartoonist position. She decided that if she was to draw another painting of something special that strikes her eye that she would find another contest to enter into it.

Being a cartoonist was not easy but Winnie loved it ever since she was a child. She used to love it until she won the prize for the waterfall painting! Turmoil about career paths, did she choose the right one? She loved painting scenic pictures but could she make a living with it? The answer was no.

Winnie stuck to being a cartoonist as it was what paid her bills. She dabbled with painting for a hobby but knew her limitations. Winnie took a reality check and knew in her heart that she was meant to be a cartoonist. Painting was something that she loved but found out it was best to stay as a hobby. Sometimes in life, interests turn into hobbies, and only sometimes do hobbies turn into life goals that could support a person's life. So in conclusion, Winnie had a very successful life as a cartoonist and painted various woodland scenes as a hobby.

PERSONAL NOTES

X plore your gut intuition in helping you understand life.

C onsider your core being with greatness; what is your gift to the world.

E stablish a center within yourself to draw your intuitive thoughts.

L et positive affirmations help you on your life's journey.

S natch the moment of connectivity with others.

I nitiate communication when at loss for words.

A spire to give to others as you would like to receive.

Chapter Twenty-Four

XCELSIA

Xcelsia was a salesperson in a famous department store in Studio City, CA. It was time to get up to go to work. She had to be in the store at 9:30 AM. Xcelsia loved being a sales person as she loved working with the public but often times had sore feet from standing on them all day. She worked over forty hours a week and had Monday's off.

One Saturday morning an old movie star came into the store and needed help. The other salesperson did not want to wait on the "Old Lady." Xcelsia recognized who the famous actress was and now was about eighty years old. She was meticulously groomed with long shiny sandy color hair that was turned under very neatly. Her make-up was expertly applied and she wore a beautiful black tapered long coat and boots. Xcelsia helped her pick out a blouse and she tried it on. She could tell by the look in her eyes that she wanted her youth back but dealt with aging gracefully. She gave the aura of a very exclusive wealthy time gone by.

As Xcelsia finished the sale, she said, "Aren't you Katherine?" with a big smile she said, "Yes." Xcelsia put the blouse in a bag with the hanger and wished her the best. When her shift was over, she asked herself, "Why did she wish the old actress the best when she was the one who needed the most?" Well, the answer came from within, she cared about people and she felt that in her heart that the "Old Actress" really needed her common blessing as meager as it was.

Xcelsia went home thinking about the incident and how their lives touched each other even for a brief moment. The actress was probably thinking about her many years of being famous and how she wished she was young again and living the excitement of being in the public's eye. Xcelsia lived every day as a salesperson and most likely will never be famous. She was also in the public's eye but in a different fashion. She helped people find what they were looking for at the store, while the actress helped people forget about life for a while when she was on stage. They both had something in common. Xcelsia and the actress Katherine, both were giving of themselves for people that they didn't personally know but happy to serve the public.

PERSONAL NOTES

Y ield what is not yours and you will have peace of mind and heart.

O ppose thoughts of greed; honesty is a winner always.

L eave your words like possessions; to someone who will appreciate them.

A rrange your will so that the right person(s) gets your belongings.

N ip the idea that more is more; you have more with less.

D estine to give others a fresh start in life when yours is over.

A rrange the finality of your wishes.

Chapter Twenty-Five

YOLANDA

Yolanda was a gardener for wealthy clients and she lived in Newport, RI. Being thirty-eight years old, she found her profession as a gardener. She loved to be outdoors with the natural elements of the sun, wind, and sky. She also loved to be with nature and the animals that lent itself to the environment. One day Yolanda was digging in the back yard flower garden of a client. Something shiny arose from the ground. She picked up a diamond ring. It was a huge diamond with a yellow gold band that was very unusual. Yolanda said, "Hmmm! The owners of this mansion would not care about this ring at all with amount of money that they have!" Yolanda decided to take the ring to an appraiser that she had heard of.

Yolanda went to the appraisers the very next day. He said the ring was valued at $500,000.00. Wow! She put it in her safe deposit box and went to work at the mansion. As luck would have it, one of the owners was there that day. Yolanda was talking to her and somehow they got on the subject of old things. The owner said that her mother used to garden in this very garden and lost her wedding ring. She went on to say that she would give anything to have it back but it was missing for over twenty years and probably would never be found.

Yolanda went home in turmoil. It must be the ring that she found yesterday! Yolanda didn't know what to do! The owner didn't need the ring or the money even if it got sold! Yolanda was thinking about things she could do with the money! She tossed and turned in her sleep. An inner voice said, "Yolanda, give the ring to the owner and tell her the truth about how you found it in the garden." Well, Yolanda called the owner the next morning and said that she wanted to see her. The owner said, "Fine, I will meet you at ten o'clock." Yolanda met the owner at ten o'clock and told her the story and gave her the ring. The owner cried, "This was Mom's ring!" The owner said, "Thank you very much for being honest." Yolanda left to start digging in the garden. Summer turned to autumn and then winter set in. Garden work grew scarce. Since Yolanda had no work, she hardly had enough money to eat and to pay her monthly expenses. She was hoping that her money would last throughout the winter but her expenses outweighed her cash.

One day she received a phone call from an attorney. The attorney said that the reading of Miss Valenti's last will and testament will be read at nine AM on Friday and her presence was requested. Yolanda was nervous about attending such a meeting. Friday came soon enough and the reading of the will started promptly at nine o'clock. No one was there except Yolanda, the attorney, the paralegal and the probate court judge. This appeared to be odd to Yolanda and she felt a cold chill up her spine.

The will had a hand written letter from Miss Valenti. It said, "Dear Yolanda, I wanted to give a test of your honesty, integrity, and truthfulness. I planted that expensive ring that you found and returned to me. It was not my mother's but just something that I had purchased. Since you returned it to me in good faith, I leave you my whole estate. Now you can hire a gardener of your own. May God speed be with you!"

PERSONAL NOTES

Z ero in on the things you love to do and what you are good at; you can follow that roadmap to be your life's work.

I nvest in a good education to help fulfill your life's work.

N otify authorities of dangerous conditions.

G arnish your life's work with love.

A spire to become your personal best and you will become it.

Chapter Twenty-Six

ZINGA

Zinga Miller hated the city and loved the country and animals. Zinga who was now forty years old knew she wanted to be a veterinarian since she was five years old. She couldn't have any pets in the apartment building where she lived in southern Sante Fe, NM and she just couldn't wait to get on with her life. Zinga achieved her goals of going to Veterinarian School, graduated, and then moved to rural Vermont to a home on a lake surrounded by woods.

Animals and wild life were very special to Zinga. She knew it was more than a job to her. It was her life. Graduating and moving to Vermont all in one month was a big transition but Zinga was ready for it. When Zinga arrived in Vermont, she started work immediately. She bought one-half of an office space and a practice from a lifelong veterinarian in Vermont. She rented a small home on a lake and was surrounded by woods. She loved the country and enjoyed skiing in the winter and swimming in the summer.

One snowy winter night, Zinga heard a noise outside of her home. She put on the floodlights and much to her surprise there was a bear trying to get into her home! She was very frightened and called 911. They laughed and thought that she was a prank caller. Zinga proceeded to quietly shut off all of the lights and tiptoe almost without breathing back to her bedroom. Slowly and quietly she got fully dressed in case she needed to be dressed for an emergency. Chills ran up her spine thinking about the danger lurking for her outside of her home. Zinga laid on her bed in a quiet stillness. While on her bed, she fell asleep.

The morning came and Zinga'a alarm startled her. She awoke and looked around for the bear. She got ready for work and when she drove the jeep to her office practice, she questioned herself if she the right choice of coming out here and all. She felt safe in her jeep and did not see any site of a bear. Much to Zinga's surprise, when she arrived at her practice, there were two emergencies. One dog and one cat who desperately needed her to operate and to stitch them up. The other animal patients were just regular check-ups. Zinga saved the cat and dog and that what is was it all about. She knew she loved the animals; she loved being a professional veterinarian; and most of all she loved the beauty of the country with its majestic color all year round and found Vermont to be her long awaited home.

PERSONAL NOTES

Your Chapter
YOUR NAME
YOUR CHAPTER

Gail J. Chiasson

I was born and raised in Connecticut. Presently, I live in Southbury, Connecticut with my husband. We have two grown children. My formal education includes an Associate in Science, a Bachelor of Science, and a Master of Science. My hobbies are sewing, home decorating, writing, yoga, and creating geometric stained glass designs.

Sewing, home decorating, and writing have been favorite hobbies of mine since childhood. Yoga has been a physical, mental, and spiritual exercise for me and I am glad to practice it, as my health is very important to me. Being an amateur stained glass artist is a magic connection for me to embellish my love of color and light.

I enjoy my family, friends, hobbies, learning new things and wrote a book of short stories to embellish my life-long ambitions.

Namaste,

Gail J. Chiasson

www.ingramcontent.com/pod-product-compliance
Lightning Source LLC
Chambersburg PA
CBHW060805050426
42449CB00008B/1543